THE WORSHIP OF GOD

GABRIEL MILLER

The Worship of God

Published by All Peoples Ministries
P.O. Box 3034
Lynchburg, Virginia 24503
www.allpeoplesministries.org

Copyright © 2018 Gabriel Miller

Cover design by Samuel Petty

ISBN-13: 978-0-9987608-1-0
ISBN-10: 0-9987608-1-0

Printed in the United States of America

To my wife, a true worshipper

CONTENTS

INTRODUCTION

My wife and I were attending the annual conference of the National Association of Schools of Music. During the final time slot, just before we were slated to check out of the hotel and drive home, we chose to sit in on the "Sacred Music" meeting. The format: two speakers followed by group discussion. One of the speakers said something akin to "the worship of Buddha is still worship." I didn't think much of it, assuming he meant what I would have meant if I had said that: we either worship God or we worship something else; one is righteous and the other is evil. During the discussion, the speaker was questioned on this stance. Without knowing any better, I stood up and tried to bridge the gap of this "simple misunderstanding." What I basically said was that in order to be clear about what we are saying, perhaps we should add adjectives like "true" and "false" to the word *worship* so that we know which type we're talking about. Then I said this: "The worship of anything not-God is idolatry."

Little did I know. Little did I know that that statement would change our lives forever. After the meeting, the Deans from Liberty University who heard me say that, struck up a conversation with us, and within seven months we were moving from Louisiana to Lynchburg, Virginia. Little did I know that that statement would also frame a pair of books that I believe God has led me to write some four years later: *The Worship of God* and *Idol Worship*. Everybody worships something or someone. And there are only two categories of worship, the worship of God and the worship of not-God. Period. Ladies and Gentlemen, it's high time that we return, with all that is within us, to the former.

This book is not meant to be a comprehensive theology of worship. It's not meant to be an in-depth history, nor a biblical chronology. All of these books have already been written, and written well. Instead, my aim here is simply to be obedient in writing down some insights into biblical worship that I believe the Lord has given me to share. This is not an overly scholarly book, and it should be accessible to the entire Christian community, including pastors, worship leaders, and laity.

In Chapter 1, we begin with the case for why we worship, arguing that it is the very purpose we were created for. An examination of what Scripture has to say about man, before the fall and after Jesus returns, shows that we were made to "glorify God and enjoy Him forever." In Chapter 2, we consider a few of the attributes of God that are most relevant to our understanding of worship. He is Trinity, which means that worship is birthed in relationship. He is good, which means that worship is a free and heartfelt response to Him, and not coerced or fear-based. And He is holy, just, and jealous, which means that our worship must be acceptable. In Chapter 3, we learn that only Christian worship qualifies as true worship of the living God. Jesus Christ is the only way to the Father. When we worship God, we are participating in the worship *of* Christ, worship *in* Christ, and worship *through* Christ. In Chapter 4, we examine the default settings of the worshipping heart toward God: wonder, adoration, and gratitude. In Chapter 5, we study the true biblical meaning of *praise*. Praise, as a subset of worship, is crucial to properly worshipping God. And biblical praise is rich and multifaceted in its meaning, stretching far beyond a simple conception of "thanksgiving through music." In Chapter 6, we take a look at the four primary words in Scripture that are translated *worship*. From this examination we conclude that biblical worship is most closely tied to the concepts of reverence and service. In Chapter 7, we note that one of the largest gaps in worship theology in our time is the omission of holiness from our vocabulary and from our lifestyles. Holiness is required of believers, and according to Scripture, living in holiness *is worship*. In Chapter 8, we are warned that deception is the primary barrier to true worship. Many believe they are worshipping God, but they have simply deceived themselves into that assumption. Ten types of deception are offered, which, it is hoped, will lead to revelation and repentance. In Chapter 9, we close by making a case for the use of music in congregational worship. We see that music is commanded in Scripture. And we work through some of the reasons why God has given such a gift for this function.

1
WHY WE WORSHIP

Oh, the depth of the riches both of the wisdom and of
the knowledge of God! How unsearchable His judg-
ments and untraceable His ways! For who has known
the mind of the Lord? Or who has been His counselor?
And who has ever given to God, that He should be
repaid? For from Him and through Him and to Him are
all things. *To Him be the glory forever.* Amen. *Therefore*,
brothers and sisters, in view of the mercies of God, I
urge you to *present* your bodies as a living sacrifice, holy
and pleasing to God; this is your true *worship*.
                                        –Romans 11:33-12:1 (CSB)

I believe this is the most significant passage on worship
in the entirety of Scripture. It tells the why, the what, and the
how of worship. For this reason it will be an overarching
backdrop to the progression of thought throughout this
book. We will return to it several times, seeing different
nuances each time. We begin, in this chapter, with the
discussion of the *why* of worship.

Worship is the very purpose you were created for. It is the most important thing you can do, and the thing, above all other things, that you must do. Of course, you must know right off that if I am attaching this level of significance to worship, I must not be talking about music, nor the first 30 minutes of church. I am not at all saying that the first half of church is the most important thing we do. So, what do I mean when I say *worship*? The Westminster Catechism sums it up nicely: *the chief end of man is to glorify God and enjoy Him forever.* For now, we'll define worship this way—glorifying God and enjoying Him forever. This is our "chief end," in other words, our primary and highest purpose.

Glorifying God

Notice the following Scriptures that indicate that the reason we were created was to glorify God.

Everyone who is called by My name, whom I have created *for my glory*; I have formed him, yes, I have made him.

–Isaiah 43:7

For you were bought at a price; *therefore glorify God* in your body and in your spirit, which are God's.

–1 Corinthians 6:20

Our Lord and God, You are worthy *to receive glory* and honor and power; *because You have created all things, and by Your will they exist and were created*."

–Revelation 4:11 (CSB)

And now returning to our opening passage from Romans, pay particular attention to the train of thought in the underlined portions:

5

(1) To God be the glory

(2) Therefore present yourselves

(3) This is your true worship

From Him and through Him and to Him are all things. It is all about Him. Period. And He receives the glory from His creation. Period. It's all for Him, and He will receive glory, whether you choose to be a part of giving Him glory or not. Since all this is the case, we are told to present ourselves. The verb of Romans 12:1 is *to present*. The *act* of worship is *presenting*. Worship is presenting yourself, a sacrifice in perpetuity, in holiness, for the glory of God.

What does that mean, to present? It's a little bit strange this command to present, isn't it? Notice it doesn't say "to God be the glory, therefore shout" or "to God be the glory, therefore preach the gospel" or "to God be the glory, therefore tithe." It says to present ourselves to God. And with that presentation comes sacrifice and holiness, which are acceptable. (We'll say more about this part later.)

I believe this word *present* is a very important word, and specifically, it's a very important word with respect to worship. It's the first step. To get a good picture of presenting, we might imagine a company of soldiers who are called to inspection. They have prepared their uniforms, polished their shoes, etc. They assemble in their appropriate military attire, they stand at attention, and they are looked over by the commanding officer. What are they doing? They are presenting themselves. Presenting is showing oneself to be ready. Once they pass inspection, they have shown themselves to be ready. At that point, they may move forward in the various tasks that they are called to perform.

This is the way we are to understand our worship of God. We first present ourselves to Him. We stand before Him, knowing that our purpose in everything we do is to give Him glory. We stand at attention and present our bodies holy and acceptable to Him. Once He walks by and passes us on our inspection, we are ready to go do things for Him. But presenting ourselves always comes first.

Sometimes it's better to think of standing *at ease*. Because our actions of worship must originate from a position of resting in His finished work. We must "be" before we can "do." That's why Jesus said "abide in Me" (Jhn 15:4). That's why Paul spoke of being seated "in the heavenly places in Christ Jesus" in Eph 2:6 *before* giving us the instructions to "walk worthy of the calling" in Eph 4:1. We must "be" before we can "do." And the "being" and the "doing," it's all worship.

Enjoying God

Enjoying God is the "take" part of our fellowship with Him in worship. We "give" when we glorify God; we "receive" when we enjoy Him forever. And it is absolutely right and proper that we should do so.

> ... who can eat and who can *enjoy* life apart from Him? For to the person who is pleasing in His sight, He gives wisdom, knowledge and *joy*...
> –Ecclesiastes 2:25-26 (CSB)

> In Your presence is fullness of *joy*. At Your right hand are pleasures forevermore.
> –Psalm 16:11

> Let them shout for *joy* and be glad, who favor my righteous cause; And let them say continually "The LORD be magnified, who has pleasure in the prosperity of His servant."
> –Psalm 35:27

Everything we have is from God. He has made the world for our enjoyment, and for His. He comforts us, He blesses us, He gives peace, He gives mercy, He answers prayer, He is our portion and our cup, our refuge, our provider. We were made to enjoy God.

In the Beginning

If we really want to understand our purpose, we might reasonably expect to find it at the beginning and at the end of the story, before the fall and after the consummation of our union with Christ. In the end we see a direct and explicit expression of glory to God: Day and night they do not rest crying "Holy, Holy, Holy" and "Worthy is the Lamb Who was slain" (Rev 4:8, 5:12). Our eternal purpose is to declare His <u>holiness</u> and His <u>worth</u>.

And in the beginning, we see a more subtle, yet still compelling picture of man's purpose. Here are 10 aspects of our purpose, 10 expectations that God has for mankind, that we can extract from the Genesis account:

(1) Imitate God. "Then God blessed them and God said to them, 'Be fruitful' ..." (Gen 1:28). The first command God gave Adam and Eve was to be fruitful. Now, fruitful, literally, means to biologically reproduce. But there was a much deeper meaning in this command that goes beyond Adam and Eve to every single one of us. To be fruitful is to be creative, to imitate God's creative acts and nature. As Paul wrote later, "Be imitators of God" (Eph 5:1). Besides the literal command for procreation, God was saying to Adam and Eve, "I just created, now you go create. I made you in my image, I made you to be creative beings, so go be creative, imitating Me in my creativity, and in so doing, I will receive glory."

8

(2) Multiply. "Be fruitful and multiply" (Gen 1:28). Part of our purpose in life is to multiply. Let me say that another way. Part of worshipping is making more worshippers. We're here to fill the earth with worshippers. If everything was only about worshipping around the throne, He could have just stopped the whole show a long time ago. He wants us to reproduce as many worshippers as we can, while we can.

(3) Walk in Power and Authority. "Fill the earth and subdue it; have dominion over the fish of the sea, over the birds of the air, and over every living thing that moves on the earth" (Gen 1:28). God receives glory through His established order, and the dominion of man over earth is part of that order. Just as the first family was expected to have dominion over the natural world, we as restored citizens of the kingdom are to have dominion in the spirit-world. Part of worshipping is walking in power and authority, and to the extent we do not walk in power and authority, we are not worshipping fully.

(4) Work. "Then the LORD God took the man and put him in the garden of Eden to tend it and keep it" (Gen 2:15). The expectation was that man was to work. When God created, He sat back and looked at His work and said "it's good." Likewise, when we work an honest toil, we get to sit back one day per week and enjoy the fruit of our labor. And God receives glory from this. Not coincidentally, the Hebrew word for *work* (cultivate, keep) in this verse, *abad*, is translated elsewhere in the Old Testament *worship*: "Worship the LORD with reverence, and rejoice with trembling" (Psa 2:11, NASB).

(5) Choose. "But of the tree of the knowledge of good and evil you shall not eat, for in the day that you eat of it you shall

surely die" (Gen 2:17). God gave Adam a choice in that garden. He clearly indicated what the right choice was. But He allowed the first couple to choose, right or wrong. God made man more than just a being. He made a person, with a will, with the power of choice. When we make choices, we are working out God's plan for creation. He receives glory from our choices. Especially when they are choices *for Him*!

(6) Obey. "But of the tree of the knowledge of good and evil you shall not eat, for in the day that you eat of it you shall surely die" (Gen 2:17). God gave a command not to eat of a certain tree. The correct choice was to obey. This test of obedience early in the pre-fall narrative shows that obedience is an important part of what we were created to do. Obedience is part of worship, and God receives glory from it.

(7) Think. "Out of the ground the LORD God formed every beast of the field and every bird of the air, and brought *them* to Adam to see what he would call them. And whatever Adam called each living creature, that was its name" (Gen 2:19). As John Lennox has pointed out, this is the first instance in Scripture of taxonomy.[1] Man observes, he categorizes, and he labels. In other words, Genesis 2:19 is God's ordination of science. All scholarly endeavors, if they are grounded in holiness, are ordained of God. Mental pursuits and the sharpening of our minds are a part of what we are supposed to do, what we were designed to do. And that brings God glory.

(8) Enjoy God. "And they heard the sound of the LORD God walking in the garden in the cool of the day, and Adam and his wife hid themselves from the presence of the LORD God

among the trees of the garden" (Gen 3:8). He came to walk with them in the cool of the day. There was a close, intimate relationship between God and man. Our original purpose was to enjoy the presence of God with a level of intimacy that we know nothing about today.

(9) Bring Acceptable Offerings. "And in the process of time it came to pass that Cain brought an offering of the fruit of the ground to the LORD. Abel also brought of the firstborn of his flock and of their fat. And the LORD respected Abel and his offering, but He did not respect Cain and his offering. And Cain was very angry, and his countenance fell" (Gen 4:3-5). For whatever reason, Cain's offering was not acceptable. Ultimately it was not acceptable because his heart was not right. "The sacrifices of God are a broken spirit, A broken and a contrite heart—These, O God, You will not despise" (Psa 51:17). When we bring acceptable offerings, with a right heart, purified by His Son, God receives glory.

(10) Experience His Presence. "And Cain said to the LORD, 'My punishment is greater than I can bear! Surely You have driven me out this day from the face of the ground; I shall be hidden from Your face; I shall be a fugitive and a vagabond on the earth, and it will happen that anyone who finds me will kill me'" (Gen 4:13-14). The original expectation was that we would experience God's presence. Even post-fall, we find that Cain experienced God's presence. When he sinned and was turned away, it was the absence of God's presence that Cain could not bear.

Whole-life Worship

Everything we do as believers is worship. We bring glory

to God through worship at our workplaces, in our physical and mental development, as we walk in obedience, as we learn to exercise our power and authority in Him, and as we enjoy His presence. If we first present ourselves to Him in full submission, everything that follows is worship. Doing the dishes is worship, changing a diaper is worship, going to work is worship, reading your Bible is worship, coming to church is worship, emptying the trash is worship, watching TV could even be worship. (Rest is ordained of God.) It is all worship IF we first present ourselves to God, if we offer it as worship. *Wherever and whenever the believer is, there is the time and place for worship.*

Perhaps nobody understood this principle any better than the greatest composer of all time, Johann Sebastian Bach. Among his many posts during his career, he was Konzertmeister for the Duke of Weimar, which was a secular position, and he was Cantor for several churches in Leipzig, which was a "sacred" position. But Bach did not differentiate between sacred and secular. Whether he composed sacred or secular music, he habitually inscribed different abbreviations at the top and bottom of his scores. J.J. for the Latin *Jesu Juva* means Jesus Help, I.N.J. for the Latin *In Nomine Jesu*, In the Name of Jesus, and S.D.G. for *Soli Deo Gloria*, to the glory of God alone. Bach understood the principle of whole-life worship.

Worship is Love

Love the Lord your God with all your heart, mind, soul, and strength (Luk 10:37). This is essentially what I have defined as *worship*. Now you may ask, well why don't you just call it *love*? And we very well could. But notice something. What I am saying is that in this passage the two words are interchangeable. To worship God IS to love God. The relationship is like that of a square and a rectangle. A square is a rectangle but a rectangle is not necessarily a square. Similarly worship is love, but love is not necessarily worship. The difference between *worship* and *love* is simply this: Love is omnidirectional, whereas worship is unidirectional. Love can emanate from God to us, or from us to God, or from us to our neighbor. It is omnidirectional. But worship is that love that is specifically emanating from us to God. God loves us, but He does not worship us. We may love our neighbor, but we do not worship our neighbor. But when we love God we are worshipping God. When we obey the first and greatest commandment, we are worshipping. This is why I say that worship is paramount to everything else. It is what Jesus Himself has called the greatest commandment. To love God with all your heart, all your soul, all your mind, and all your strength is your primary purpose. This is worship.

2
THE GOD WE WORSHIP

Consider these thoughts from the opening of A.W. Tozer's classic work *The Knowledge of the Holy*:

What comes to your mind when you think about God is the most important thing about you.

Worship is pure or base as the worshipper entertains high or low thoughts of God.

The idolatrous heart assumes that God is other than He is—in itself a monstrous sin—and substitutes for the true God one made after its own likeness.

The essence of idolatry is the entertainment of thoughts about God that are unworthy of Him.

Wrong ideas about God are not only the fountain from which the polluted waters of idolatry flow; they are themselves idolatrous. The idolater simply imagines things about God and acts as if they are true.

The heaviest obligation lying upon the Christian Church today is to purify and elevate her concept of God until it is once more worthy of Him—and of her. In all her prayers and labors this should have first place.[2]

To understand the worship of God, we must have an accurate picture of the God we worship. We can say we worship God, but if the God we worship does not look like, sound like, and act like the God of Scripture, we are not worshipping God at all. Tozer goes on to lay out some doctrine on several of the attributes of God, as have many other authors. Among the attributes, God is: Self-existent, Self-sufficient, Eternal, Infinite, Immutable, Omniscient, Omnipotent, Omnipresent, Transcendent, Immanent, Good, Just, Merciful, Gracious, Holy, and Sovereign. It's not within the scope of this work to build a comprehensive doctrine of God here (as if I even could). But I do want to point out a few things about God that I believe are important for understanding worship.

God is Trinity

Understanding who God is begins with the knowledge that He is Three-in-One. Why is this so foundational? Because as a triune Being, *God is inherently relational.* God is in relationship with Himself. This, of course, is impossible for us to fully comprehend, just as it's impossible for us to fully comprehend God's existence outside of (not before) time. But we must try to picture it for a moment. "In the beginning, God created the heavens and the earth" (Gen 1:1). That means the beginning was the beginning of time and space and matter. Since it was the beginning of time, there was no "before," and yet God "existed." So what did it look like for God to exist "then" (which is not really then because there's no time)? We don't know. But what we do know is that

Father, Son, and Holy Spirit live in a state of eternal fellowship. A constant state of ecstasy. God is pure love and pure joy, and that love and joy spring from His complete satisfaction in and of Himself.

Out of the overflow of His self-relationship, He Created. God created, not because He needed us, nor because our presence in any way makes Him happier or more fulfilled, for He is infinitely happy and fulfilled in and of Himself. But rather He created simply because he wanted to share the ecstasy of relationship with others. When we share in this relationship, He receives glory.

> That which we have seen and heard we declare to you, that you also may have fellowship with us; and truly our fellowship is with the Father, and with His Son Jesus Christ.
>
> -1 John 1:3

When we understand that God is a relational Being whose sole purpose in creating us was to allow us to share fellowship with Him, we begin to entertain the right perspective on worship. *Worship is participation in right relationship with God.* It is fellowshipping with God. It is relating to God appropriately. So what are the appropriate ways to relate to God? Jesus lays them out for us in the Lord's Prayer.

Our Father which art in heaven. This line refers to the *Father-son relationship.*[3] And it is not by chance that it comes first. We must begin our worship from the position of resting in the affirmation of the Father. Abba Father, Daddy God, is proud of you. When you mess up, He does not bat an eye. He is there to help you get back on track. He will correct you, but

He always corrects out of love. When we understand God as Father, we are secure in identity, and free to move forward from that "resting place" (Eph 2:6) into any and every mission we are called to.

Hallowed be Thy name. This line refers to the *Holy-profane relationship*. More precisely, the Holy-profane dichotomy, because the holy and the profane cannot be in relationship. A holy God cannot commune with a profane people. That's why He sent His Son as a substitutionary atonement, to take our profanity onto Himself, that we could become holy. When we understand that God is holy and we are not, we are awed and humbled, and we seek to be holy as He is holy, by allowing Him to develop His holiness in us.

Thy kingdom come. This line refers to the *King-subject relationship*. God is the King. And there are rules of engagement for fellowship between a king and his subjects. There is a protocol, there is a reverence, there is a respect. But God is also the King of kings, and we're the kings. So "Thy kingdom come" also refers to the King-king relationship. We are God's delegated authorities on this earth. We have dominion. We are tasked with the advancement of the kingdom, and we have the full authority of the Creator behind us.

Thy will be done, on earth as it is in heaven. This line refers to the *Master-slave relationship*. He bought us, we belong to Him, and we have to do what He says. Slavery is just as much an aspect of the Christian walk as sonship is. They are two different aspects. They are both true. And they are not contradictory. We have many rights and privileges as His sons, but we also have many important responsibilities as His slaves.

Give us this day our daily bread. This line refers to the *Provider-dependent relationship.* All good gifts come from God. Sometimes we can trick ourselves into thinking that we take care of ourselves. We put food on the table, we put clothes on our families' backs. Yes, but all of that ultimately comes from God. You wouldn't have your needs met, no matter how hard you worked, if God had not ordained that they be met.

And forgive us our trespasses, as we forgive those who trespass against us. Here we have the *Forgiver-transgressor relationship.* We have transgressed a holy God. And yet He has offered forgiveness, a forgiveness that was unimaginably costly to Him. Because He forgives us, we are told to forgive others. And this, too, is part of worship.

Lead us not into temptation. This line refers to the *Leader-follower relationship.* He leads us beside still waters. He restores our souls (Psa 23:2-3). When we consider God as Leader, we see His lovingkindness, trusting that He will never lead us astray. "For as many as are led by the Spirit of God, these are sons of God" (Rom 8:14). The Holy Spirit is our constant companion, leading us and guiding us into all truth and holiness.

But deliver us from evil. This line refers to the *Deliverer-freedman relationship.* He is our Savior. He is our Hero. He has saved us, He is saving us, and He will save us. We pray daily for Him to deliver us from the evils of the day. And He is faithful to do just that!

God is Good

"The goodness of God leads you to repentance," writes Paul in Romans 2:4. True worship is a response to His goodness. That means:

(1) True worship is not coerced. Yes, God is sovereign, but He does not force us to worship Him. In His sovereignty, He has ordained that we have the power to choose whether or not we will serve Him. Our worship should never come from a place of obligation. It should not be laborious, it should not be drudgery. It should be a glorious and joyful response to the limitless mercy of a wonderful Savior. Now, that is not to say that there won't be times when we may not feel like worshipping, and we nevertheless push through with a sacrificial offering of worship. But this sacrifice is more a response to circumstances than it is a response to God, and it should not be the norm. A worship that is freely and cheerfully given is the appropriate response to a good God.

(2) True worship is not undertaken for the purpose of getting something in return. Yes, God rewards those who diligently seek Him (Heb 11:6), but this is not the basis on which we worship Him. The theology being taught in many circles today is that we worship God for what we can get out of it. That is a very dangerous road. The so-called prosperity gospel forgets that the purpose of worship is to glorify God, not to glorify us. Now, I make no apologies for being a believer in prosperity (by which I do not mean that exorbitant amounts of wealth are normative). I believe God wants us to prosper as our soul prospers (3Jo 2). But—and this is a very important but—our prosperity is a fringe benefit of a life of dedication to God, it is not the reason we worship, it is not an ulterior motive. Seek ye first the kingdom, not seek ye first the prosperity (Mat 6:33). A true response to the goodness of

God is always humbling, never selfish.

(3) True worship is not done out of fear. Yes, God is to be feared. "It is a fearful thing to fall into the hands of the living God" (Heb 10:31). And if I have to err, I would rather err on the side of fearing God than on the side of approaching God with flippancy. However, the response to God's goodness, worship, is an acceptance of an invitation that He has lovingly presented to us. He sent His Son, Who was tortured and killed on our behalf. By His blood we are told we can "come boldly to the throne of grace" (Heb 4:16) and obtain mercy! We don't worship God because we're afraid of what will happen if we don't. We worship Him because He has flooded us with goodness.

God is Holy and Just and Jealous

God's *holiness* means He is completely other. He is totally different from His creation. We are made in His likeness, which means we are like Him, but He is not like us. Part of His otherness is His total sinlessness. We really can't comprehend this, but His sinlessness makes His being, His essence, completely removed and distinct from our being, our essence. God's *justice* means that all final verdicts must be true. It means He will not let anything slide, every score will be settled, every intricate detail. God's *jealousy* means that He has a strong desire to see His people walk worthily of Him. He has established the covenant of our marriage—the marriage of Christ and His Church—and He expects us to be faithful.

God's holiness, justice, and jealousy, together lead us to conclude one thing: *He will not abide unacceptable worship.* His holiness will not allow it, His justice will not allow it, and His jealousy will not allow it. The worship of God must be *acceptable.* So, how do we ensure that our worship is acceptable? That is the subject of the next chapter.

3

CHRISTIAN WORSHIP

When you are sick and need medicine, there are some medicines that you can simply go into a drugstore and purchase. And there are other medicines that require a prescription. You must go to a doctor and receive a prescription in order to have access to that medicine. So it is with worship. You can worship anything and anyone you want, at any time. Idolatry is over-the-counter. But the worship of God requires a prescription. In ancient times, the prescription included brazen altars and animal sacrifices. But this was just a temporary prescription that really never did kill the root disease. "For it is not possible that the blood of bulls and goats could take away sins" (Heb 10:4). Instead, these were patterns of the real prescription that followed, *Jesus Christ*. Jesus said, "I am the way, the truth, and the life. No one comes to the Father except through Me" (Jhn 14:6). The worship of God is prescription medication, and the prescription is Christ. Only through Christ can the worship of

God be accomplished. Without Christ, all worship is idol worship. With Christ, the worship of God—what we now may call Christian Worship—is accomplished.

Of Christ

We worship the triune God, which means we worship the Father, we worship the Son, and we worship the Spirit. When God is the object of worship, the Father is the object of worship, the Son is the object of worship, and the Spirit is the object of worship. This means that, in part, the worship of God is *the worship of Christ*. We see this bear out several places in Scripture. The wise men came to worship the newborn King. Not the Father and not the Spirit. They worshipped the Son. Mary anointed the feet of Jesus with ointment of spikenard. Doubting Thomas—whom I like to refer to as Believing Thomas because he made some of the statements of greatest faith in the entire Bible!—when He saw the risen Lord, bowed down and exclaimed "My Lord and my God!" Notice Jesus didn't correct these folks. It was (and is) right and proper that Jesus receive worship.

It is the Lamb that is worshipped in Revelation 5:8-9. The word that is used to describe the Lamb in verse 9 is *worthy*. That word, in Greek, is *axios*. It is not the same word used, for example, when John the Baptist says he's not worthy to loosen His sandal strap (Luk 3:16). That word is *hikanos*, and it means *deserving*. John was not deserving of that honor. But *axios* doesn't mean that. It means worth-y, in other words, valuable. It is derived from the concept of balancing scales, on which an item is placed on each side, and they are determined to be of equal (or unequal) weight. *Axios* is the same word used to indicate that a laborer is worthy of his wages (1Ti 5:18); the amount of work is equal to the pay. So when we see that the Lamb is worthy, *axios*, in Revelation 5:9, it is literally saying that the sacrifice of Christ has balanced out my sin on the divine scales of justice! He is worth-y! And because He is worth-y, He is to receive my worth-ship.

In Christ

The worship of God is accomplished *in Christ*. John records that the Word was made flesh and dwelt among us (Jhn 1:14). That word *dwelt* literally means *He pitched His tent*. In describing Jesus this way, John is (I believe, purposefully) referring us back to the Mosaic tabernacle. God instructed Moses to build a tabernacle, a tent, where His presence would rest, and worship would take place. Jesus' incarnation is the fulfillment of that presence in the tabernacle. Jesus similarly identifies Himself as the temple in the next chapter: "Destroy this temple, and in three days I will raise it up" (Jhn 2:19).

So we see that Jesus replaces the tabernacle in the Mosaic worship model and he replaces the temple in the Davidic worship model.[4] This means, as the true tabernacle, Jesus is the "tent of meeting" for us and God, and as the true temple, Jesus is the "place where worship occurs." The worship of God is worship that is accomplished *in Christ*.

Through Christ

Perhaps most importantly, the worship of God is worship that is accomplished *through Christ*. Jesus is called in various places throughout the New Testament *the door, the gate, the way*, and so on. It is Jesus that we must go through to participate in the worship of God. He is the prescription. And He is the ONLY prescription. "No one comes to the Father but by Me," He said.

"There is one God and one Mediator between God and

man, the Man Christ Jesus" (1Ti 2:5). Jesus is our mediator. That means He intervenes on our behalf. He is our advocate, according to 1 John 2:1. That means He's our lawyer; He pleads our case to the Father on our behalf.

And finally, Jesus is the Word. This means that He is the communicative force of the Trinity, and the communicative agent between us and God. Trinitarian relationship is accomplished through Him. And the relationship between us and God is accomplished through Him. He is the only way we have of communicating with God. Our relationship with God grows as we communicate with Him, and communication is only possible through Him, the Word. Worship is participation in right relationship with God. Salvation is not, and has never been, the "end-game." It's the "beginning-game." Fellowship is the end-game. How do we develop fellowship? Communication! The Word! *The cross made relationship possible; communication makes relationship palpable.*

4
THE DISPOSITIONS OF THE WORSHIPPER

I have two boys, 7 and 4. Depending on the day and time, they may manifest various moods or attitudes. They may be excited for one reason at one time, and disappointed for another reason at another time. They also display a variety of actions. Sometimes they are very loving and cuddly. Sometimes they are more distant and interested in their "things." But underlying their ever-changing moods and actions is a fairly consistent *disposition*. It is what defines our relationship. Underneath the surface, they know who I am, and they know who they are, and they operate out of this knowledge of relationship. They know I love them, and because of that, they love me. They know I mean business, and because of that, they respect me (and most often obey me). They know I have never let them down, and because of that, they trust me.

As a relationship grows, the underpinning of that

relationship becomes more constant. It is this underpinning, this constant, that I am calling *dispositions*. So what are the dispositions of the worshipper? Not the moods or attitudes or feelings, not the thoughts or actions, but the unchanging "setting" from which our actions flow? If I am a worshipper, what should I find my default perspectives toward God to look like? What are my instinctive responses to God? What is the natural inclination of my heart toward God? Or more precisely, what is the *supernatural* inclination of a true worshipper's heart toward God?

Wonder

The first disposition of the worshipper is *wonder*. The worshipper looks upon God with a complete sense of awe, which in turn produces reverence and fear, leading to humility. When we gaze upon God and His works we should readily develop a sense of wonder.

It was wonder that caused Moses to make haste in bowing his head to the earth in worship, as the full glory of the LORD passed by his sheltered soul in the cleft of the rock. It was wonder that left Isaiah completely broken when he beheld the fullness of God's holiness, and realized its total incompatibility with his sin. It was wonder that gave Job the answer he had been searching for through his painful trial, when the voice of God thundered down the rhetorical questions of spiritual calibration:

> Where were you when I laid the foundations of the earth? ... Who determined its measurements? ... To what were its foundations fastened? Or who laid its cornerstone[?] ... Have you commanded the morning since your days began? ... Where is the way to the dwelling of light? Can you send out lightnings, that they

may go, and say to you 'Here we are!'? Who has put wisdom in the mind? Or who has given understanding to the heart?

–Job 38:4-6,12,19,35-36

"I have heard of You by the hearing of the ear," Job says. "But now my eye sees you. Therefore I abhor myself, and repent in dust and ashes" (Job 42:5-6).

It was wonder that a blinded Saul displayed on the road to Damascus. It was wonder that an incapacitated John felt on the Isle of Patmos. It is wonder that we will one day understand fully, and enjoy forever. And it is wonder that we must seek here in the temporal.

It can be sought. And many have sought and found wonder in days past. The Archbishop of Canterbury, Anselm, found it in the 11th century. In his *Book of Meditations and Prayers*, he writes:

> When I consider what God is, how sweet His Being, how loveable, and how good; when I think how It baffles all resources of speech and all capacity of wonder, and what demands It makes on the reverence and the admiration of every creature; and when, on the other hand, I see and understand what man is, whom very God made to His own Image and Likeness, and whom, furthermore, He created such that as he should always display in himself the image of the Creator, so he might always keep in mind the will and the love of Him who made him such as he is; when I review all this, I am overcome with wonder and astonishment at the inestimable goodness of the Creator God ...[5]

The great hymnist Isaac Watts found wonder in the 17th century. No doubt he was overcome with it when he penned this verse:

Adore and tremble, for our God
Is a consuming fire!
His jealous eyes his wrath inflame,
And raise his vengeance higher.

Almighty vengeance, how it burns!
How bright his fury glows!
Vast magazines of plagues and storms
Lie treasured for his foes.

Those heaps of wrath, by slow degrees,
Are forced into a flame;
But kindled, oh! how fierce they blaze!
And rend all nature's frame.

At his approach the mountains flee,
And seek a wat'ry grave;
The frighted sea makes haste away,
And shrinks up every wave.

Through air so wide the weighty rocks
Are swift as hailstones hurled;
Who dares engage his fiery rage
That shakes the solid world?

Yet, mighty God, thy sovereign grace
Sits regent on the throne;
The refuge of thy chosen race
When wrath comes rushing down.

Thy hand shall on rebellious kings
A fiery tempest pour,
While we beneath thy shelt'ring wings
Thy just revenge adore.

Thy just revenge *adore*. Wonder leads to the second
disposition of the worshipper:

Adoration

Adoration encompasses longing and desire, admiration, excitement and delight. These are among the instinctive responses to a real relationship with God.

David understood this. He was a man who adored his God. He writes:

> O God, You are my God;
> Early will I seek You;
> My soul thirsts for You;
> My flesh longs for You
> In a dry and thirsty land
> Where there is no water.
> So I have looked for You in the sanctuary,
> To see Your power and Your glory.
> Because Your lovingkindness is better than life,
> My lips shall praise You.
> Thus I will bless You while I live;
> I will lift up my hands in Your name.
> My soul shall be satisfied as with marrow and fatness,
> And my mouth shall praise You with joyful lips.
> When I remember You on my bed,
> I meditate on You in the night watches,
> Because You have been my help,
> Therefore in the shadow of Your wings I will rejoice.
> My soul follows close behind You;
> Your right hand upholds me.
>
> —Psalm 63:1-8

Solomon understood adoration, too. He portrayed it differently. The *Song of Solomon* gives us insight into the biblical celebration of love between man and woman, and it serves as a metaphor for the adoration we should feel for God. In this dialog between the bride and groom the woman exclaims, "Take me with you—let's hurry! Oh, that the king would bring me to his chambers" (Sng 1:4, CSB).

There is excitement, anticipation, and expectation of intimacy in this tone. God wants us to long for Him and desire Him like a bride anticipates her groom. Now it is important to note here that the bride in Song of Solomon is analogous to the corporate church, the singular Bride of Christ. There is no sense in which our individual relationships with God are in any way romantic. But they are intimate. Meaning that God desires to be close to us, for us to know Him as He is. The true worshipper reciprocates this desire.

For the individual believer (as opposed to the corporate church), what intimacy with God entails is sitting on Daddy's lap. This is the picture Paul paints in Galatians 4 and Romans 8 when he uses the term "Abba, Father." He says "we are sons of God" and "we seek to climb up on God's lap and say 'Dada!'"

Now, for those who have not had a good relationship with their earthly father, this can be difficult. As it may be difficult for those with bad marriage experiences to relate to the Christ-Bride picture. We must understand, however, that we cannot project our earthly view of fatherhood (or marriage) onto God. God is the Creator. Everything is reflective of Him; He is not reflective of it. It is absolutely backward to try to understand God the Father by projecting our idea of fatherhood onto Him, good, bad, or indifferent. Rather, we begin to understand what it means for us to be fathers when we observe God as Father.[6]

And similarly, a man should love his wife "just as Christ also loved the church and gave Himself for her" (Eph 5:25). As husbands, we are to follow the model of Christ. He does not follow the model of us. We are not to project our idea of marriage onto the union of Christ with His Church. We are to recognize the *agape* love of Christ for His Church, and apply that love to our own marriages. So, it is not, in fact, as I contended earlier that "God wants us to long for Him and desire Him <u>like</u> a bride anticipates her groom." Just the opposite, the excitement and longing the bride has for her groom is <u>like</u> the desire the corporate church feels for Christ.

So, adoration is a disposition of the worshipping heart toward God. It is not developed. It is a gift from God, and it is a gift we should earnestly desire. It is a gift that He wishes to freely give. He merely waits for us to seek Him out. Many have sought Him and found Him, and in finding Him have been given a deep adoration for Him.

Frederick Faber was given an adoring heart in the 19th century. His disposition toward God flowed from his heart through pen to paper as he crafted this artistic expression of loving awe:

> The thought of God, the thought of Thee
>   Who liest in my heart,
> And yet beyond imagined space
>   Outstretched and present art:
> It is a thought which ever makes
>   Life's sweetest smiles from tears;
> And is a daybreak to our hopes,
>   A sunset to our fears
> It is not of His wondrous works
>   Nor even that He is
> Words fail it but it is a thought
>   That by itself is bliss
> The very thinking of the thought
>   Without a praise or prayer
> Gives light to know and life to do
>   And marvellous strength to bear

And Anselm, once again, reveals the abundance of his heart when he records his 14th Meditation:

Be with me now, O God; You whom I seek, whom I love, whom I confess with heart and mouth, and adore with all my powers. My mind, bound by all vows to You, inflamed with love of You, breathing after You, yearning after You, longing to see You and You only, knows no other sweetness than to speak of You, hear of You, write of You, speculate on You, and muse anon on Your glory in the heart's deepest depth, that the sweet thought of You may be some little solace and repose to me in the midst of the whirl and turmoil of this present state. You, therefore, I invoke, O most desired Lord; to You I cry with a mighty cry in my inmost heart...

You, O Lord, fill heaven and earth; sustaining all things, but without effort; filling all things, but without contraction of Yourself; ever active, yet ever at rest; gathering together, yet needing nothing; seeking, though You lack nothing; loving, but without distraction; jealous, yet free from care. You repent, but are never sorry; You are angry, yet undisturbed. You change Your dealings, but alter not Your purpose. You recover what You find, and You have never lost. Never in want, yet You rejoice in gain. Never greedy, yet You demand a costly price. You pay in excess to whom You owe nothing, and ever receive in excess, but only so that You may owe. And who has anything that is not Yours? ... You are everywhere, and everywhere are entire. Perceived You may be, but You can never be seen. In no place are You otherwise than present, and yet You are far from the thoughts of the unjust. Nor are You absent in the place from which You are far removed; for You are not there to bless, but You are there to punish. Unmoved and unmoving do You stand, and yet we follow after You, and following cannot overtake You. You hold all things, fill all things, enfold all things, surpass all things, and sustain all things. You teach the hearts of the faithful without sound of words. Undisturbed by reach of distance, unchanged by lapse of time, tideless and ebbless, You

make the inaccessible light Your dwelling, … At rest
and self-sustained, nevertheless You forever encircle
all. You cannot be parted and divided, for You are truly
one; nor are You here, and there, and there again; but
You, in your Triunity, enfold all, fulfill all, enlighten all
and possess all.[7]

He enfolds us, fulfills us, enlightens us, and possesses us. For
this, we have no other course but to be thankful. This
becomes the third disposition of the worshipper:

Gratitude

I will say less on the subject of gratitude. There is little
more to say other than because of the great love God has
shown to us, it is befitting and essential that we should
respond instinctively to Him with gratitude. We are not
talking about *giving* thanks or *demonstrating* thanks or *saying*
"thanks," though these are important. We are talking about
the thankful*ness* that is the source of these expressions. But
this disposition of gratitude is unnatural for fallen, sinful man.
Just the opposite, the natural disposition of fallen man is
entitlement.

So gratitude is not something we are born with, and it is
not something we can work up to. The disposition of
gratitude is very much a gift from God. It is a gift that we
need. And it is a gift that we should ask Him for.

Others have asked, and others have received. The great
church father, Augustine, was given a grateful heart in the 4th
century. In his book of *Confessions* he writes:

O my God, let me, with thanksgiving, remember, and
confess to You Your mercies on me. Let my bones be
soaked in Your love, and let them say to You, "Who is
like You, O Lord? You have broken my bonds in pieces;

I will offer unto You the sacrifice of thanksgiving." And how You have broken them, I will declare; and all who worship You, when they hear this, will say, "Blessed be the Lord, in heaven and in earth, great and wonderful is His name."[8]

And let us not assume that only the great, famous men of God are the ones who have manifested a heart of wonder, adoration, and gratitude toward the Most High. God can and does place these dispositions in the heart of *any* believer who pursues Him fervently. In the 18th century, a young, spiritually lukewarm John Wesley learned this one night when he crossed paths with a poor, unremarkable fellow working on the Oxford campus. On the cold night, Wesley admonished the man to go home to retrieve a better coat.

"I thank God for this *one* coat I possess," replied the man. "And I thank Him for water, which is my only drink during the day." With his heart seized, Wesley probed deeper, "What else are you thankful for?" "I thank Him," the man said, "that He has given me my life and being, a heart to love Him, and a desire to serve Him."[9]

A desire to *serve* Him. Wonder, leading to adoration, leading to gratitude, all reinforcing our position in relation to God, the low position, looking up, not the high and exalted position, looking down. The dispositions of the worshipping heart relegate it to complete submission, and from these dispositions spring the actions that define the very essence of the worshipper: the actions we call *service*.

"I beseech you therefore, brethren, by the mercies of God, that you present your bodies a living sacrifice, holy, acceptable to God, which is your reasonable *service* ... your true *worship*."
–Romans 12:1 (NKJV and CSB combined)

THE WORSHIP OF GOD

A Prayer

Our Father in heaven, we confess to You our shortcomings. We have not wondered a wonder proportionate to Your glory; we have not adored an adoration commensurate with Your love; we have not thanked a thanksgiving sufficient to requite Your blessings. The dispositions of the worshipper are not native to our sin nature, but they are in the Spirit nature that You have implanted in us. Kindle this flame, and fan it. Develop within us hearts that see You for Who You are: all in all. Make us true worshippers. We trust You to make it so, for we believe that You desire to do so, and we know that only You can. Amen.

5
BIBLICAL PRAISE

Ok, it's finally time to get into the nuts and bolts of worship. What is it exactly? And how do we go about doing it, and doing it biblically? One word that is often tied to worship—and rightfully so—is *praise*. We can think of praise as a subset of worship. All praise is worship, but not all worship is praise. Praise is declaring something, and praise is expressing something. Praise involves our mouths, whether spoken or sung or shouted. And praise involves several different postures, including bowing and kneeling and even raising our hands. In this chapter we'll get a better understanding of biblical praise. Then we'll return to the broader concept of biblical worship in the following chapter.

Some Common Assumptions

The modern church generally conceives of *praise* as synonymous with *thanksgiving*. This is not a bad start. Three of the Hebrew words translated *praise* in the Old Testament denote the concept of giving thanks, at least in part. Thinking of praise as thanksgiving can lead to another popular belief that we *praise* Him *for what He has done*, but we *worship* Him *for who He is*. This, too, is partially true, although the Hebrew word *tehillah* encompasses both concepts at once. It is a praise demanded by His deeds, qualities, or attributes. In other words, we *tehillah* Him for what He has done *and* for who He is.

Many also conceive of praise as being specifically tied to music, particularly in the church service. Also true. Several of the Hebrew words translated *praise* are in some way tied to music-making, whether singing or playing instruments. The New Testament echoes these concepts of praise. Words such as *ainos*, *aineo*, and *hymneo* denote such ideas as singing the praise of, extoling, lauding, and singing praises in honor of God.

Seven Hebrew Words for Praise

So we have a pretty good starting point for understanding praise, but the meaning of biblical praise is far deeper and richer than just thanksgiving and music. Let's take a closer look now at each of the seven most common Hebrew words for praise, in order to broaden and strengthen our overall concept of biblical praise.

- *Towdah*

Towdah occurs 32 times in the Old Testament. Of these occurrences, it is translated *praise* 6 times (and it is translated *thanksgiving* 18 times).[10] It means:[11]

- thanksgiving
- thanksgiving in songs of liturgical worship

38

- sacrifice of thanksgiving
- confession

Here are some examples of how *towdah* is used in Scripture:

Offer to God *towdah*, and pay your vows to the Most High.

–Psalm 50:14

Whoever offers *towdah* glorifies Me; And to him who orders his conduct aright I will show the salvation of God.

–Psalm 50:23

Enter His gates with *towdah*, and into His courts with praise. Be thankful unto Him, and bless His name.

–Psalm 100:4

• *Tehillah*

I have already mentioned *tehillah*, and the added dimension it carries that we praise God for Who He is, not just for what He has done. Here are the other shades of meaning for this word:

- song or hymn of praise
- adoration
- thanksgiving paid to God
- praise demanded by the attributes or deeds of God
- renown, fame, glory
- the person or thing wherein anyone glories

Tehillah occurs 57 times in Scripture, and it is translated *praise* all 57 times. Here are a few examples of its usage.

He is your *tehillah*, and He is your God, Who has done

for you these great and awesome things which your eyes have seen.

–Deuteronomy 10:21

I will bless the Lord at all times; His *tehillah* shall continually be in my mouth.

–Psalm 34:1

Enter His gates with thanksgiving, and into His courts with *tehillah*. Be thankful unto Him, and bless His name.

–Psalm 100:4

Two more references are particularly enlightening. First, notice that we are told to *tehillah* "in the assembly of the saints" in Psalm 149:1. This is one of several words that is prescribed for usage in what we would now call the church service. Second, notice the result of this example of *tehillah*:

And when he [Jehoshaphat] had consulted with the people, he appointed those who should sing to the LORD, and who should praise the beauty of holiness, as they went out before the army and were saying: "Praise the LORD, For His mercy endures forever." Now when they began to sing and to *tehillah*, the LORD set ambushes against the people of Ammon, Moab, and Mount Seir, who had come against Judah; and they were defeated.

-2 Chronicles 20:21-22

Here we see that *tehillah* praise was actually the key to victory in battle! When we praise the Lord, He traps our enemies and defeats them. Biblical praise is a key to the victorious life!

• *Barak*

Barak is not translated praise at all in the KJV, but it is translated praise several times in the NIV and some other translations. Most often, in fact in 302 of its 330 occurrences, it is translated *bless*. The word means:

- to bless
- to kneel
- to be blessed
- to be adored

Here are some examples of its usage:

Barak be the LORD, Who daily loads us with benefits, the God of our salvation!

–Psalm 68:19

For You, O LORD, will *barak* the righteous; with favor You will surround him as with a shield.

–Psalm 5:12

Barak the LORD, O my soul, and forget not all His benefits:

–Psalm 103:2

Lift up your hands in the sanctuary, and *barak* the LORD.

–Psalm 134:2

My foot stands in an even place; in the congregations I will *barak* the LORD.

–Psalm 26:12

Oh come, let us worship and bow down: let us *barak* [translated *kneel*] before the LORD our maker.

–Psalm 95:6

The last three once again show that praise is to be done "in the sanctuary," among "the congregations." We also see that

THE WORSHIP OF GOD

barak praise can imply kneeling, which adds another posture or expression to our collection.

• *Shabach*

Shabach is another Hebrew word translated *praise*. And it has a multidimensional meaning. It can mean:

- to laud, to commend
- to soothe, to still
- to address in a loud tone
- triumphant praise

In other words, to shout. God has created us to shout His praise! "Shout to God with the voice of triumph!" we read in Psalm 47:1. (The word *shout* in that particular verse is not *shabach*, but another Hebrew word. Nevertheless, the point is, it is commanded!)

Shabach occurs 11 times in Scripture, and of those, it is translated praise 6 times. Note some of its various usages:

> Because Your lovingkindness is better than life, My lips shall *shabach* You.
>
> —Psalm 63:3

> You rule the raging of the sea; When its waves rise, You *shabach* [translated *still*] them.
>
> —Psalm 89:9

> A fool vents all his feelings: but a wise man *shabach* [translated *holds them back*].
>
> —Proverbs 29:11

> Praise the LORD, all you Gentiles! *Shabach* Him, all you peoples!
>
> —Psalm 117:1

- *Zamar*

Zamar is the word for *praise* that is most closely tied to music. It occurs 45 times in Scripture, and is translated *praise* 26 of those times. The other 19 times it is translated *sing* or *sing psalms* or *sing forth*. It can mean:

- sing; sing praise
- make music
- play a musical instrument

Here are some examples of its biblical usage:

> *Zamar* the LORD, who dwells in Zion! Declare His deeds among the people.
>
> —Psalm 9:11

> It is good to give thanks to the LORD, And to *zamar* Your name, O Most High;
>
> —Psalm 92:1

> Praise the LORD, for the LORD is good; *zamar* His name, for it is pleasant.
>
> —Psalm 135:3

- *Yadah*

So far we have seen thanksgiving, music, postures such as kneeling, and expressions like singing and shouting, all combining into a pretty robust concept of biblical praise. The two remaining words, which are also two of the words most frequently translated praise, add many more shades of meaning to our understanding of praise. For this reason, I really want to take a little extra time to discuss them.

The Hebrew word *yadah* occurs 114 times in the Old Testament, and it is translated *praise* 53 times. But unlike the five words we just examined, *yadah* has a much deeper and richer meaning. Its spiritual meaning derives from its physical meaning, which connotes a throwing or casting motion. Here are its myriad shades of meaning:

- to throw
- to cast; to cast down; to throw down (as a stone)
- to shoot (as arrows)
- to confess sin; to show oneself guilty
- to give thanks
- to profess
- to point out with the hand extended

In other words, *yadah* praise is one of the biblical foundations for the worship expression of hand-raising. When we complete a throwing motion, we must at some point during that motion find ourselves extending the hand upward. I have always heard it taught that we raise our hands in surrender to God (as if at gunpoint), and this is essentially correct (except for the gunpoint part). We are surrendering our sins and our concerns to God, who alone is able to forgive and soothe. But when we do this, we are not just surrendering, we are praising, we are *yadah*-ing. And that hand-raising has two functions. First, the concept of 'casting' should bring to mind the familiar practice of "casting all your care upon Him" because He cares for us (1Pe 5:7). To praise in this sense is to cast our burdens, our shortcomings on Him, as there is no other way to rid ourselves of them. We confess our sin, we throw our guilt upon Him. He is our Savior, and He has taken all of our sin and shame upon Himself. *Yadah* praise is the physical symbolic act of us celebrating the substitutionary atonement. We demonstrate to ourselves and to God in this

44

throwing motion, that we surrender our sin and guilt to Him Who died to become, and subsequently extinguish, sin and guilt (2Co 5:21, Gal 3:13).

The second function of hand-raising found in the meaning of *yadah* is the "pointing out" aspect. We "point out with the hand extended" the One Who is worthy of praise, the One Who takes away our sin and guilt. Biblical hand-raising is not just raising but also pointing. *Yadah* praise is throwing our sin onto God, and pointing out the God Who saves from that sin.

Here are a few examples of *yadah*'s use in Scripture:

> I will make Your name to be remembered in all generations; therefore the people shall *yadah* You forever and ever.
>
> -Psalm 45:17

> When a man or woman commits any sin that men commit in unfaithfulness against the LORD, and that person is guilty, then he shall *yadah* [translated *confess*] the sin which he has committed. He shall make restitution for his trespass in full, plus one-fifth of it, and give it to the one he has wronged.
>
> –Numbers 5:6-7

> And the heavens will *yadah* Your wonders, O LORD; Your faithfulness also in the assembly of the saints.
>
> –Psalm 89:5

> Let the peoples *yadah* You, O God; let all the peoples *yadah* Thee.
>
> -Psalm 67:3

> Enter into His gates with thanksgiving and into His courts with *yadah*. Be thankful unto Him and bless His name.
>
> -Psalm 100:4

We are commanded to *yadah* God. And *yadah* means "point out with the hand extended." So lifting hands in praise is not just a gimmick, it's a command. Paul echoes this sentiment in the New Testament when he writes: "I desire therefore that men pray everywhere, lifting up holy hands, without wrath and doubting" (1Ti 2:8). And the Psalmist confirms it even more plainly: "Lift up your hands in the sanctuary, and bless the LORD" (Psa 134:2).

I hope that this little discussion has given you an understanding of the biblical foundations of hand-raising. It's not just something for more expressive worshippers to draw attention to themselves. It's for everyone, and it's biblical. If we know and understand that raising our hands signifies admission of guilt, the symbolic casting of our sin onto God, and pointing out He who is our Savior, the gesture will have meaning, and we can employ it biblically and worshipfully.

• *Halal*

By far the most common Hebrew word for *praise* in the Old Testament is *halal*. It's also my favorite. Of its 165 occurrences in Scripture, it is translated *praise* 117 times. It is one of the root words in *hallelujah*, meaning *praise the LORD*. But it also means:

- to shine, to flash forth light, to make bright or shining
- to boast, to be boastful
- to be praiseworthy
- to make a fool of, to act madly, to act like a madman
- to be clear, to be brilliant (as of a sharp tone)

Here are some examples of how it is used in Scripture:

I will declare Your name to My brethren; In the midst of the assembly I will *halal* You.

—Psalm 22:22

Do not *halal* [translated *boast*] about tomorrow, For you do not know what a day may bring forth.

—Proverbs 27:1

Halal Him, sun and moon; *Halal* Him, all you stars of light!

—Psalm 148:3

So he changed his behavior before them, *halal[ed]* [translated *pretended madness*] in their hands, scratched on the doors of the gate, and let his saliva fall down on his beard.

—1 Samuel 21:13

Let me first say a word about this last passage. You may recall that the context of this is when David was on the run from Saul, and found himself under the scrutiny of King Achish of Gath, who was not too keen on David being there. When David got wind of the king's displeasure at his presence, he *halal*[ed], which is to say he pretended to be insane, acting like a madman. Many will say it is a stretch to apply this shade of meaning of the word *halal* in the context of praise. But I'm not so sure. That same David gives us another example, in which he praised the Lord, we might say 'like a madman.'

Now as the ark of the LORD came into the City of David, Michal, Saul's daughter, looked through a window and saw King David leaping and whirling before the LORD; and she despised him in her heart.

Then David returned to bless his household. And Michal the daughter of Saul came out to meet David, and said, "How glorious was the king of Israel today, uncovering himself today in the eyes of the maids of his servants, as one of the base fellows shamelessly uncovers himself!"

So David said to Michal, "It was before the LORD, who chose me instead of your father and all his house, to appoint me ruler over the people of the LORD, over Israel. Therefore I will play music before the LORD. And I will be even more undignified than this, and will be humble in my own sight. But as for the maidservants of whom you have spoken, by them I will be held in honor.

Therefore Michal the daughter of Saul had no children to the day of her death.

–2 Samuel 6:16, 20-23

The word *halal* is not used in this passage to describe David's demonstrative praise, but clearly it was extravagant, undignified, and in that day and setting, a bit crazy. I'm not sure how far to bring this idea into modern day praise and worship, but I will leave you with this warning. What is physical in the Old Covenant often becomes spiritual in the New Covenant. Do not despise those who would dare to praise extravagantly. You may find yourself spiritually barren.

Now let me say a bit more on another aspect of the meaning of *halal*. It means to shine or flash forth light. In other words to glow with the light of God. I like to think of this concept in terms of two metaphors. First, *halal* praise is like a pregnant lady who gives off a radiant glow. There is something inside her, a life, that shines through her in a way that is essentially out of her control. The joyful glow of the pregnant lady is evidence and testimony of the source. Second, *halal* praise is like the moon reflecting the light of the sun. The moon gives off light not of its own power, but reflecting the only true source of light. It shines in the darkness.

True life producing true light, reflected off impotent

satellites incapable of producing light of their own power, and shining filtered as a sign of the source of light: this is the image of *halal* praise that emerges. And it is an image that is reinforced and amplified in the New Testament. John 1:4 proclaims that in Jesus "was life, and the life was the light of men." Jesus is "the true light" (Jhn 1:9) and we reflect His light to the world (Mat 5:14). In this sense, being the light of the world is itself a form of praise. This passive form of praise, which is to say an uncontrollable consequence of receiving the Holy Spirit by faith, is given kinetic energy by our active demonstrative praise, whether in private or in a corporate worship setting. When we sing, shout, give thanks, raise our hands, or participate in any other kind of active praise, we are simply consciously expressing in those discrete moments the continuous praise that proceeds from our lives as believers, the reflection in radiant glow of the true Light.

Praise is a Command

The active gestures and expressions of praise found in Scripture are not optional. All seven of the words we have just studied are presented as commandments to believers. We are not always given specifics about when or where or how often to do these things. But we are told to do them. Consider the following directives from the Psalms.

Towdah

Offer to God *towdah praise*, and pay your vows to the Most High.

–Psalm 50:14

Tehillah

Rejoice in the LORD, O you righteous! For *tehillah praise* from the upright is beautiful.

–Psalm 33:1

Zamar

Shout joyfully to the LORD, all the earth; Break forth in song, rejoice and sing *zamar praises*.

–Psalm 98:4

Barak

Lift up your hands in the sanctuary, and *barak praise* the LORD.

–Psalm 134:2

Shabach

Shabach Praise the LORD, all you Gentiles! Laud Him, all you peoples!

–Psalm 117:1

Yadah

Oh, *yadah praise* the LORD, for He is good! For His mercy endures forever.

–1 Chronicles 16:34

Halal

Halal praise the LORD! *Halal praise* God in His sanctuary; *Halal praise* Him in his mighty firmament! *Halal praise* Him for His mighty acts; *Halal praise* Him for his excellent greatness!

–Psalm 150:1-2

Just for fun, let's see how that last one would read by substituting the various meanings for *halal* into the text:

Shine with the light of the LORD. *Act like a madman for* God in His sanctuary; *flash forth His light* in His mighty heavens. *Boast in* Him for His mighty acts; *glow with his radiance* for His excellent greatness!

Praise is a command. These verses command us to give thanks, sing, confess, adore, shout, make music with instruments, lift our hands, bless, kneel, laud, commend, cast our sin and guilt, point out, profess, shine, act like madmen, boast, and glow for God. Amen!

6
BIBLICAL WORSHIP

Like praise, many believers think of worship as an event within the church service that is connected with music. This is a gross understatement of the depth of meaning of the word *worship*. You may have heard it said that worship is a lifestyle, or that everything we do is to be done in worship. These kinds of phrases are much closer to the mark.

To Ascribe Worth

Worship comes from the Old English *weorthscipe*, which means *to ascribe worth*. *Worship* and *worthy* therefore come from the same root, *worth*. The relationship is simply this: *we worship what is worthy, we ascribe worth to what is worth something*. Those things that are worth-y, or valuable, or invaluable, are those things to which we ascribe worth. Spiritually speaking, God is worthy, or infinitely valuable, and therefore we should worship—ascribe worth to—Him.

But what constitutes worship? What constitutes ascribing

worth? A brief look at the things we value and how we show that we value them will provide a simple answer to this question. The things that we value are the things that we spend time with, spend money on, make sacrifices for, enjoy, talk to or talk about. Thus, it seems reasonable to assume that these are some of the ways that we ascribe worth. To whom or what do these actions apply? Spouse? Kids? TV? Social Media? Work? To the extent we ascribe worth to these things and people in this way, we worship them in the Old English sense of the word. This is not necessarily wrong (idol worship) unless this type of worship is out of balance in our lives. But the question of worshipping God can be answered the same way. We ascribe worth to God when we spend time with Him, spend money on Him, make sacrifices for Him, enjoy Him, talk to Him and talk about Him. To the extent we don't do these things, we are not worshipping God.

To Bow

Several Hebrew and Greek words are translated *worship* in the Bible. But there are four (two Hebrew and two Greek) that are by far the most common. The first two are the Hebrew word *shachah* and the Greek word *proskuneo*. Interestingly, they mean essentially the same thing: to bow, or more specifically, to lie flat on your face. Specifically, *shachah* means to bow down, to fall down flat, to show deference or reverence. *Proskuneo* similarly means to prostrate oneself in homage to, to do reverence to, to adore, to kiss the hand (like a dog licking a master's hand), to defer to superior rank, to kneel and touch the ground with the forehead in reverence.

These are the words translated *worship*! Our first Biblical piece to the puzzle of what it means to worship God is *to bow down before Him*! Well, let me just stop right there and say that, given the extensive use of these words in the Bible, we should probably be doing a lot more of this. *Shachah* occurs 172 times in the Old Testament, where it is translated *worship* 99 of those times. *Proskuneo* occurs 60 times in the New Testament, where it is translated *worship* all 60 times. Here are some exemplary passages that show that indeed we are commanded to bow before God in worship:

> And Abraham said to his young men, "Stay here with the donkey; the lad and I will go yonder and *shachah*, and we will come back to you.
>
> –Genesis 22:5

> So the people believed; and when they heard that the LORD had visited the children of Israel and that He had looked on their affliction, then they bowed their heads and *shachah*.
>
> –Exodus 4:31

> So David arose from the ground, washed and anointed himself, and changed his clothes; and he went into the house of the LORD and *shachah*.
>
> –2 Samuel 12:20

> O *shachah* the LORD in the beauty of holiness! Tremble before Him, all the earth.
>
> –Psalm 96:9

> But the hour is coming, and now is, when the true worshipers will *proskuneo* the Father in spirit and truth; for the Father is seeking such to *proskuneo* Him.
>
> –John 4:23

> The twenty-four elders fall down before Him who sits on the throne and *proskuneo* Him who lives forever and ever ...
>
> –Revelation 4:10

Perhaps more important than the physical act of bowing, however, is the impetus behind it. It is the reverence, the respect, the fear, the awe of the otherness of God that leads these Bible characters to bow before God in worship.

To Serve

Shachah and *proskuneo* show us that a central component of worship is reverence. The two other Bible words most commonly translated *worship*, the Hebrew *abad* and the Greek *latreuo/latreia*, show us that worship also means *servitude*. *Abad* means: to serve, to be enslaved to, to do service to. Of its 290 occurrences in the Old Testament, it is most often translated *serve*. It is not translated *worship* at all in the KJV, but it is translated *worship* or *worshipers* 12 times in the NASB. *Latreuo* and its related form *latreia* mean to minister to God, to render religious homage, to serve, to do service to. Of their combined 26 occurrences in the New Testament, they are translated *worship* or *worshiper* 6 times in the NASB. They are most often translated *to serve* or *service*. Here are some examples of the use of *abad* and *latreuo/latreia* in Scripture:

> The LORD God took the man and placed him in the garden of Eden to *abad* [translated *work*] it and watch over it.
>
> –Genesis 2:15 (CSB)

> You shall fear only the LORD your God and *abad* [translated *serve*] Him, and shall take oaths in His name.
> –Deuteronomy 6:13

> Now, summon all the prophets of Baal, and his *abad* [translated *worshipers*] and all his priests; let no one be missing, for I have a great sacrifice for Baal; whoever is

missing shall not live." But Jehu did it in cunning, so that he might destroy the *abad* [translated *worshipers*] of Baal.

–2 Kings 10:19 (NASB)

Abad the LORD with reverence, And rejoice with trembling.

–Psalm 2:11 (NASB)

Then Jesus said to him, "Go, Satan! For it is written, 'You shall *proskuneo* [translated *worship*] the LORD your God, and *latreuo* [translated *serve*] Him only.'"

–Matthew 4:10 (NASB)

For we are the circumcision, who *latreuo* [translated *worship*] God in the Spirit, rejoice in Christ Jesus, and have no confidence in the flesh ...

-Philippians 3:3

Therefore I urge you, brethren, by the mercies of God, to present your bodies a living and holy sacrifice, acceptable to God, which is your spiritual service of *latreia* [translated *worship*].

–Romans 12:1 (NASB)

Worshipping God requires more than words, it requires a life of service to Him. In this sense, worship is synonymous with the essence of the true Christian walk: being a slave to Christ. The host of New Testament writers who describe themselves as "slaves to Christ" attests to the definitively Christian nature of this attitude (Rom 1:1, Jam 1:1, 2Pe 1:1, Jud 1:1, Rev 1:1). Paul explains of his commitment to the spirit over the flesh, "I die daily" (1Co 15:31). John the Baptist states it a different way: "He must increase, but I must decrease" (Jhn 3:30). Our "true worship," according to Romans 12:1, is the offering of our bodies as "*living sacrifices, holy and pleasing to God.*" A life of servitude to God, a daily commitment to sacrifice our own wants in favor of doing what God wants: this is worship.

An Expanded Concept of Worship

Weaving our English, Hebrew, and Greek concepts of worship into one overarching thought now, we might arrive at a definition like this: **Worship is declaring, expressing, and demonstrating to God in reverence and servitude that He is worth more to you than is anyone or anything else.** First, we can *declare* our worship to God, ascribing worth to Him verbally. Singing, shouting, crying, talking about or talking to God: these are all ways we can declare His worth. Second, we can *express* our worship to God. Out of our reverence of His otherness, we can bow, lay prostrate, kneel, run and jump in *halal* praise, lift our hands in *yadah* praise, or simply enjoy Him. But declaring and expressing is mere lip-service if we do not, third, *demonstrate* our worship to God in servitude. Demonstration of our service to God would include giving financially, giving of time to the spiritual disciplines of prayer and the study of the Word, regular attendance in church, helping others, giving 100% effort to the daily tasks we have been charged with (work, school, etc.), sacrifice, obedience, or any other activity that glorifies God. In doing these things we worship God, not in discrete moments, but continuously, not as an event, but as a lifestyle. *A life of worship is a life of living proof that God is worth more to you than anything else is.*

7
A FOUR-LETTER WORD

> Therefore, brothers and sisters, in view of the mercies of God, I urge you to present your bodies as a living sacrifice, holy and pleasing to God; this is your true worship.
>
> –Romans 12:1 (CSB)

Romans 12:1 is a very special verse. It is a conclusion, as we can clearly see from the word *therefore*. But a conclusion to what? First of all, it is the conclusion of the main idea of the letter, which tracks from chapter 3 to chapter 5 to chapter 8 to chapter 12. That main idea is this: (1) There is no one righteous; (2) But God sent His Son, and through His propitiation we have redemption, justification, righteousness, peace, reconciliation, salvation, and no condemnation; (3) Therefore!

It's also the conclusion of Romans 11:33-36, the idea we opened this book with: (1) The purpose of everything is to bring God glory, (2) Therefore present yourselves, (3) This is worship. Framing the text in this way certainly helps us to understand the importance of worship. What it doesn't do is highlight the weightiness of the most important word in the verse. It's a word we don't hear often from our pulpits in this day and age. Consequently, it's a word that's ignored by millions of professing Christians worldwide. We have no problem applying it to God, but we get nervous when anyone suggests we apply it to ourselves. The word is *holy*. People of God, we must understand this: *holiness is not legalism, it's not inconsequential, it's not unattainable, and it's not optional.* And to realize its significance, we must examine the third thought-track that culminates in Romans 12:1—that of Romans 6-7.

The Defense of Holiness: Romans 6-7

Romans 6 and 7 serve as an "aside," in which Paul defends himself against a hypothetical question: "Shall we go on sinning so that grace may more abound?" He believes such a question might arise on the heels of his previous assertion that the effect of Jesus' righteous act completely trumps the effect of Adam's unrighteous act, such that "where sin abounded, grace abounded much more" (Rom 5:20). Of course the answer to Paul's question is an emphatic NO! Yet he doesn't think it's sufficient to provide a one-word answer. To Paul, it is so important an issue that he takes two chapters to thoroughly answer this question before returning to the main idea in chapter 8. And here is what he says:

> What shall we say then? Shall we continue in sin that grace may abound? Certainly not! How shall we who died to sin live any longer in it? Or do you not know that as many of us as were baptized into Christ Jesus were baptized into His death? Therefore we were buried with Him through baptism into death, that just as Christ was raised from the dead by the glory of the

Father, even so we also should walk in newness of life.

For if we have been united together in the likeness of His death, certainly we also shall be in the likeness of His resurrection, knowing this, that our old man was crucified with Him, that the body of sin might be done away with, that we should no longer be slaves of sin. For he who has died has been freed from sin. Now if we died with Christ, we believe that we shall also live with Him, knowing that Christ, having been raised from the dead, dies no more. Death no longer has dominion over Him. For the death that He died, He died to sin once for all; but the life that He lives, He lives to God. Likewise you also, reckon yourselves to be dead indeed to sin, but alive to God in Christ Jesus our Lord.

–Romans 6:1-11

The entire thrust of this passage is that we are joined with Christ in *both* death and life. True believers in Christ Jesus are dead to sin, and therefore can no longer live in sin (v.3). But we are also alive unto God (v.11). Well what does that mean for us? Paul continues to explain:

Therefore do not let sin reign in your mortal body, that you should obey it in its lusts. And do not present your members as instruments of unrighteousness to sin, but present yourselves to God as being alive from the dead, and your members as instruments of righteousness to God. For sin shall not have dominion over you, for you are not under law but under grace.

–Romans 6:12-14

Ah! Sin does not have dominion over us! That's what it means to be alive unto God. The life we receive gives us the power to overcome sin! John Wesley spoke of sin in three ways: the *guilt* of sin, the *power* of sin, and the *being* of sin (that is, the capacity to sin).[12] The blood of Jesus has defeated two of the three. Believers in Jesus receive grace to justify and

60

grace to empower. Through His death the *guilt* of sin is erased, and through His life the *power* of sin is erased. The capacity to sin remains, however. But Romans 6:14 makes it clear that sin does not have dominion over us, and therefore that we have no excuse to not walk uprightly before the Lord.

Now, there's something else really important here. Remember that word *present* from Romans 12:1? Ok, now notice how much Paul talks about presenting in Romans 6. He begins in verse 13: "do not *present* your members as instruments of unrighteousness," but "*present* your members as instruments of righteousness." Now he continues:

> What then? Shall we sin because we are not under law but under grace? Certainly not! Do you not know that to whom you <u>present</u> yourselves slaves to obey, you are that one's slaves whom you obey, whether of sin leading to death, or of obedience leading to righteousness? But God be thanked that though you were slaves of sin, yet you obeyed from the heart that form of doctrine to which you were delivered. And having been set free from sin, you became slaves of righteousness. I speak in human terms because of the weakness of your flesh. For just as you <u>presented</u> your members as slaves of uncleanness, and of lawlessness leading to more lawlessness, so now <u>present</u> your members as slaves of righteousness for holiness.
>
> For when you were slaves of sin, you were free in regard to righteousness. What fruit did you have then in the things of which you are now ashamed? For the end of those things is death. But now having been set free from sin, and having become slaves of God, you have your fruit to holiness, and the end, everlasting life. For the wages of sin is death, but the gift of God is eternal life in Christ Jesus our Lord.
>
> -Romans 6:15-23

If you present your members to sin to obey, you are on the road to death (v.16), but if you present your members to obedience, you are on the road to life (v.16). We used to do the former, but Paul exhorts us to now do the latter, "present your members as slaves of righteousness for holiness" (v. 19). This will produce the fruit of holiness, which culminates in eternal life. Presenting our members as slaves of righteousness, leading to holiness, leading to eternal life. Notice it does not say "responding to an altar call leads to eternal life." Now I'm all for altar calls, and I believe they can be life-changing. But what I am not for is the idea that we can say a little prayer that basically amounts to a magic spell, walk away unchanged, and somehow that constitutes salvation. No, my friend, Jesus died for much more than that. His sacrifice was unspeakably horrific. He didn't endure that so that we could wave a figurative wand, continue sinning, and believe that our grotesque behavior is "OK" because it's "covered." Church, do not be deceived, we do not simply "accept Christ" and then go on living as if nothing has changed. True believers must walk in holiness.

Now, once again, *presenting* leads to *holiness* which leads to *eternal life*. "Therefore present" Paul writes in Romans 12:1. It is the conclusion to this theme of *presenting* woven throughout chapter 6. Since it is so important that we present our members as slaves to righteousness, Paul pleads with us to present our bodies as a sacrifice of holiness. *This is worship.*

The more immediate follow-up to Romans 6 is, of course, Romans 7, in which Paul goes on to describe the war between the flesh (that is the carnal nature, not the physical body) and the spirit. His flesh is predisposed to sin, as is ours (7:25), but his mind knows what is right, and desires to follow that path. Consequently, he is engaged in a constant battle, the battle to overcome the flesh and operate in the spirit, according to the Spirit. I am quite sure that the sins he confesses in verses 15-20 are not any sins that we would consider to be of a "grave nature." He's not doing any of the things he is telling others not to do, for example. He's not committing sexual immorality or drunkenness or lewdness or any of the other "list sins" found elsewhere in the New Testament. In fact he admonishes the Corinthians that they were being carnal just to be picking sides between himself and Apollos (1Co 3:4), something we probably wouldn't even think of as sinful today. No folks, the sins that Paul struggles with are likely sins of his thought life, thoughts that he desires to control and squash, but that he's never quite able to get complete victory over. For instance, he probably thinks pretty highly of himself from time to time. Wouldn't you if you were him? And he catches himself, and he says to himself, "Oh God, no! I am the worst of all sinners! Look at the horrific acts I committed in Your name. How could I ever even for a moment be satisfied with myself and think that I am something good?!" And he repents of that, and he knows deep down that all of his goodness only comes from God, and the Spirit puts his flesh in check, and he has won another battle. I would suggest that most of the sins that Paul grieves over, the average Christian would not even consider to be sin.

The Condition for Romans 8

Once Paul makes it all the way through his aside, he's ready to go back and continue his main idea:

> There is therefore now no condemnation to those who are in Christ Jesus, who do not walk according to the flesh, but according to the Spirit.
>
> –Romans 8:1

Did you catch that little condition on the back end of that? For a long time, I never did. It doesn't occur in every translation. It was left out of several of the early manuscripts, and some translations include it while others don't. But just in case you're worried I'll build a doctrine off of an erroneous text, you should know that the phrase is repeated verbatim in verse 4:

> For the law of the Spirit of life in Christ Jesus has made me free from the law of sin and death. For what the law could not do in that it was weak through the flesh, God did by sending His own Son in the likeness of sinful flesh, that the righteous requirement of the law might be fulfilled in us who do not walk according to the flesh but according to the Spirit.
> –Romans 8:2-4

Romans 8:1-4 carries a great promise with a great condition. No condemnation! What a wonderful thing! But ladies and gentlemen that freedom from condemnation only exists for those who are in Christ Jesus. And those who are in Christ Jesus are those who do not walk according to the flesh, but according to the Spirit. (This truth found in Chapter 8 is the first landing point of the Romans 6-7 thought-track. The second is the aforementioned Romans 12:1.) We must not walk according to the flesh, and we must walk according to the Spirit. Ok, good, so what does it mean to walk according to the flesh, and what does it mean to walk according to the Spirit? Paul answers:

> For those who live according to the flesh set their minds on the things of the flesh, but those who live according to the Spirit, the things of the Spirit.
> –Romans 8:5

What is your mind set on, friend? If it is set on the things of the flesh, I strongly encourage you to examine yourself to determine whether you are in the faith (2Co 13:5). If you are in the faith, and yet you would confess that your mind is set on the things of the flesh way too often, your response right now should be one of contrition and repentance. You should be thinking to yourself, "Wow! I really want this life of holiness! I am falling short, but I want to be right." You may not even totally know how to do it, but the desire should be there to move toward holiness. Now, here is the good news! Jesus' sacrifice is all you need to make that change! He has done the work, and He will do the work through you! This message is not discouraging, it is wholly encouraging! You have the power within you to overcome sin! By faith, begin to walk according to the Spirit today, in Jesus' name!

My Own Response to a Hypothetical Challenge

At this point I can hear some screaming "Foul!" Perhaps even "heresy." Let me try to put your minds at ease. No, I really am not preaching legalism. People have been scared of legalism for so long that they don't even know what it is. Believe me I'm way "inside" of John Wesley on this (actually, don't believe me, just read what he wrote and you'll see), and even further inside his spiritual descendants who took the concept of holiness to the extreme of requiring certain hairstyles and dress code and other silliness.

I do not believe that our works save us. And nothing in this chapter should be read or interpreted in that way. The difference here is one of cause and effect. The doctrine of works-based salvation says that my salvation is the effect, and my works are the cause. That is heresy, and I don't believe it one bit! The doctrine of holiness says something quite different: redemption is the cause, and holiness is the effect.

When we examine ourselves to see if we are in the faith, the idea is not to say "because I see evidence of holy living, I know I am saved." (This is what got the Pharisees in trouble.) No, the point is, rather, to say, if applicable, "because I *don't* see evidence of holiness, I must wrestle with the possibility that I have deceived myself into a false faith." This is scriptural (2Co 13:5), and it should probably be a much more frequent pursuit.

8
DECEPTION

He also told this parable to some who trusted in themselves that they were righteous and looked down on everyone else: "Two men went up to the temple complex to pray, one a Pharisee and the other a tax collector. The Pharisee was standing and praying like this about himself: 'God, I thank You that I'm not like other people—greedy, unrighteous, adulterers, or even like this tax collector. I fast twice a week; I give a tenth of everything I get.'

"But the tax collector, standing far off, would not even raise his eyes to heaven but kept striking his chest and saying, 'God, have mercy on me, a sinner!' I tell you, this one went down to his house justified rather than the other; because everyone who exalts himself will be humbled, but the one who humbles himself will be exalted."

–Luke 18:9-14 (CSB)

The Pharisee in this parable thought he was something that he was not. He was deceived about himself. He did all the right things. He went to church regularly. He paid tithes. He fasted and prayed. To put it in modern parlance, he did not drink or smoke or swear. He may have even had self-control. But his worship was unacceptable because he was deceived about His relationship with God.

We can know all about worship, we can do all the acts of service, we can assume all the postures and employ all the expressions of worship, we can have a correct theology, we can even write books on worship—we can do all of these things and yet still not worship acceptably because of a deceived mind. *Deception is the primary barrier to worship.* That's why I thought it was important, in this book on worship, not only to talk about what worship is and how to engage in it properly, but also to warn against those things that can extinguish our ability to offer worship that is acceptable. On that note, let's consider ten ways that deception prevents us from worshipping acceptably.

Deception About Sin

The Pharisee was deceived about the fact that he was a sinner. He said, "I'm not like other people," which means he saw the sin in others without seeing it in himself. Because he couldn't point to a sin by name, he was under the impression that he was without sin. But according to Scripture, "There is none righteous, no, not one" (Rom 3:10). "All have sinned, and fall short of the glory of God" (Rom 3:23). Therefore, "If we say that we have no sin, we deceive ourselves, and the truth is not in us" (1Jo 1:8).

> Now the works of the flesh are obvious: sexual immorality, moral impurity, promiscuity, idolatry, sorcery, hatreds, strife, jealousy, outbursts of anger, selfish ambitions, dissensions, factions, envy, drunken-

ness, carousing, and anything similar. I am warning you about these things—as I warned you before—that those who practice such things will not inherit the kingdom of God.

–Galatians 5:19-21 (CSB)

Will not inherit the kingdom of God! How many are in deception about sin today? We have been taught to walk down the aisle and say a little prayer for salvation. But we have not been taught that true salvation entails the power to overcome sin! Young men, you cannot habitually engage with pornography, and then walk in on the Lord's Day, and present an acceptable offering of worship. It can't be done. We kind of look at sexual sin as the biggie, because it's so obvious. But we can't go out and wallow in gluttony all week either, or consistently lose our tempers, or look on others with jealous eyes, or throw fuel on the fire of the rumor mill. We are deceived if we believe we can do those things, and still be acceptable when we walk into the Lord's House. Now, "If we confess our sins, He is faithful and just to forgive" and cleanse (1Jo 1:9). But I'm afraid we have too many in the church today who really don't confess, really don't repent, and really don't have any intention of turning from evil and running toward God. These poor souls are deceived, and their worship is unacceptable. *To the degree you are operating in sin, you are not worshipping acceptably.*

Deception About Pride

The Pharisee reveals his pride when he states that he is "not like other people." Not only does he not see that he is a sinner just like everyone else, he actually views himself as superior to everyone else.

We often think of a prideful person as a braggart. But

most of the time that person is more insecure than prideful. James 4 explains the true nature of pride and humility:

> …God resists the proud, but gives grace to the humble. Therefore submit to God …
>
> –James 4:6-7

Therefore, submit. The distinction between pride and humility is one of submission. Humility is submission; pride is living unsubmitted. You can't do everything you want; you have to do what God wants. "Adopt the same attitude as that of Christ Jesus, who … humbled Himself" (Phl 2:5-8, CSB).

> Then Jesus said to His disciples, "If anyone wants to come with Me, he must deny himself, and take up his cross, and follow Me.
>
> –Matthew 16:24

He has redeemed us, purchased us as slaves. He is Lord, He is Master. We must do what He says. *To the degree you are operating in pride, unsubmitted to God, you are not worshipping acceptably.*

Deception About Complacency

There are things that we have to do. If you are only hearing the word, and not doing it, according to James 1:22, you deceive yourself. Jesus found fault with the church at Laodicea. They said "we are wealthy and have need of nothing." But they didn't know that they were "wretched, miserable, poor, blind, and naked" (Rev 3:17). They were deceived. Jesus said, in Matthew 7:21, that only those who do the will of the Father will enter the kingdom of heaven. *To the degree you are operating in complacency, you are not worshipping acceptably.*

Deception About Wrong Desires

The Pharisee probably thought his desires were pure. He probably thought that he desired to serve God through all of his works. He had most likely lost the tenderness that would be able to recognize when his motives veered off course. And, like those Paul discusses in Romans 1, he suppressed the truth until God likely gave him over to his depraved mind.

Wrong desires are so easy to embrace, and so easy to become deceived about. Notice these warnings about wrong desires from James:

> Friendship with the world is enmity with God.
>
> –James 4:4

> For where envy and self-seeking exist, confusion and every evil thing are there.
>
> –James 3:16

1) Friendship with the world: What does your life look like? Does it look like everyone else's life? Social media to be popular and sound enlightened, clothes and jewelry to achieve "the look," selfies to promote the self and seek approval of man. What the world finds funny should be different from what we find funny. What the world finds appealing should be different from what we find appealing "Do not love the world or the things in the world. If anyone loves the world, the love of the Father is not in him" (1Jo 2:15). Now, we are in the world, and there will, no doubt, be some overlap between our lives and the life of the world. But what James and John are saying here is: *To the degree you are operating in friendship with the world, you are not worshipping acceptably.*

2) Envy: Is there anyone you are jealous of? Do you covet your neighbor's stuff? Do you covet your neighbor's life? Do you covet your neighbor's talent? Do you covet your neighbor's callings or giftings? Do you covet your neighbor's ministry? *To the degree you are operating in envy, you are not worshipping acceptably.*

3) Selfish ambition: Do you want to be great? Do you want to be famous? Do you want your church to be famous? Do you want your ministry to be famous? Notice, there's a big difference between successful and famous. Success is doing whatever God says no matter the outcome. Sometimes that results in fame, sometimes not. Until we truly get to the place where we don't even *want* the credit, much less care who gets it, our heart is not fully devoted to Him. What is our real motivation in desiring the things of God? Is it so we can *be used* for His glory, or is it just for His glory to come, whether we're used or not, whether we're recognized or not? *To the degree you are operating in selfish ambition, you are not worshipping acceptably.*

Deception About Misplaced Trust

The parable of the Pharisee and the Tax Collector was told to those "who trusted in themselves." We say we trust in God, but do we really? It is easy to say we trust in God when we have a job, and the rent is paid, and we're operating in the black every month. Some readers may have experienced the kind of lack that forces one to trust God when the money wasn't there, when the food wasn't on the table, when the paycheck was not coming in every other week. Others have never been tested in that way.

One litmus test about where your trust is placed is to examine your plans. Do you plan everything out? Do you get stressed out when things don't go according to your plan?

Now I am not saying that we should never plan, and that we should just go through life willy-nilly with no direction. But if you are relying on your plans to determine your future at the expense of listening to God's direction for your life, you have misplaced trust. The Chaldeans in Habakkuk 1:11 incur guilt because "their strength is their God" (CSB). Have we placed our own abilities, our own work ethic, our own ideas, our own strength above God? *To the degree you are operating in misplaced trust, you are not worshipping acceptably.*

Deception About Works

This is an oldie but a goodie. It is among the most basic of Christian tenets: we are saved by faith, not by works. But many of us still operate in a works-based mindset. And we are so deceived about it we don't even realize it. The Pharisee didn't realize it. He said, "I fast twice a week; I give a tenth of everything I get." He was counting on his works to save him. Jesus said that many would say "Lord, Lord" and yet not enter the kingdom (Mat 7:22-23). Why? Because they are deceived and believe that it is the things they are doing that will save them. Do you count on your tithe to keep you in good stead with God? Do you count on your prayer life and fasting? Luke 18:12 says that doesn't move you closer to God. There is only one way to get to God, only one mediator between God and man—and that is the Man Christ Jesus (1Ti 2:5). *To the degree you are operating in a works-based mentality, you are not worshipping acceptably.*

Deception About Feelings

Here we are speaking of the warm-fuzzies of the church experience. When we have a true encounter with God, there will be conviction, fear, reverence, and a changed heart with consequent actions. (See Isaiah 6, Exodus 3, Revelation 1, and Acts 9.) That is not to say that feelings are bad, or that we can't have an emotional connection to or reaction to God. God created us as emotional beings, and He expects us to be emotional, especially when it comes to our relationship with Him. But if it's *only* emotional, and not life-changing, it is not pure, deep, worship. If your life is not changing, if you're not growing, it doesn't matter if you get "the feeling" every Sunday, you're not a worshipper. *To the degree you are operating in feelings to the exclusion of the life-changing power of the Spirit, you are not worshipping acceptably.*

Deception About Unforgiveness

This one is big, and it's very scary. Notice the gravity of this statement:

> And when you stand praying, if you have anything against anyone, forgive him, that your Father in heaven may also forgive you your trespasses. But if you do not forgive, neither will your Father in heaven forgive your trespasses.
>
> –Mark 11:25-26

Are you harboring unforgiveness? You've got to let it go. No matter how badly you've been hurt, God expects forgiveness because He forgave. However badly you have been hurt, God was hurt worse by your sin. And forgiving only relieves the burden, it never increases it. Forgiveness is good for you! Receive God's grace today to fully forgive your offender in Jesus' name! This supernatural power is part of your inheritance as a believer! And friend, if you don't walk in it, according to Mark 11:26, you're in big trouble. *To the degree you are operating in unforgiveness, you are not worshipping acceptably.*

Deception About Guilt

Here we are speaking of the idea of a blood-bought believer who lives in an unbiblical self-imposed oppression of guilt and condemnation. Even though we know this is not the correct outlook, we often dismiss this deception as "not all that bad." People who live in guilt are viewed as victims; we feel sorry for them; we wish they could snap out of it. But we don't really see this as a sin. We see it as an unfortunate attitude, but not as a wrong attitude. But it *is* a wrong attitude. Consider this, *a person who lives in guilt is living in a perpetual state of denying Christ's sacrifice.* Living in guilt is saying "I know Jesus died for my sins, but I'm not willing to accept that it's all paid for." Living in guilt leaves Jesus on the cross. It ignores the finished work. It ignores the resurrection and ascension. Acceptance of a state of guilt is rejection of your rightful ownership of a not-guilty verdict, a state of innocence. How can you worship the Savior if you are rejecting the validity of the salvation!? Living in guilt and condemnation is a very dangerous thing. And make no mistake, *to the degree you are operating in guilt and condemnation, you are not worshipping acceptably.*

Deception About Brotherly Love

The Parable of the Pharisee and The Tax Collector was told to those who "looked down on everyone else." Loving your neighbor as yourself is not optional (Luk 10:27). Are we really doing this, or have we deceived ourselves into thinking we are when we're really not? Now we can go too far with this. I don't think we're supposed to be mowing our neighbors lawns every Saturday, cooking them dinner every night, and paying all of their bills, although we can do some of those things some of the time, as the Lord leads. But do you really care about people? Do you care about others as you care for yourself? Do you take on the burdens and the cares of others as if they were yours? Do you pray for others, not just yourself? Do you see others as equally important and valuable before the Father, or do you view yourself as better than others?

> If someone says, "I love God," and hates his brother, he is a liar;
>
> –1 John 4:20a

> Pure and undefiled religion before God and the Father is this: to visit orphans and widows in their trouble, and to keep oneself unspotted from the world.
>
> –James 1:27

Now, on the other hand, some suffer from feelings of inferiority. You feel that you are worse than everyone else. Everyone is more important than you. *Love your neighbor as yourself* implies that you have love for yourself. Feelings of inferiority are as wrong as feelings of superiority, because we are all equally valuable to God.

Friends, let's purpose to love ourselves and love one another as ourselves, for this is the outworking of loving God. This is worship. And, *to the degree you are not loving your neighbor as you love yourself, you are not worshipping acceptably.*

9
THE PROPER ROLE OF MUSIC
IN WORSHIP

Well we've almost made it to the end of a book on worship, and I've said very little about music. But if you've read the first eight chapters you know that the reason why is that music really has little to do with worship. The word *worship* in Scripture primarily means bowing down and serving, and it is never tied to music explicitly. So what, then, is the proper role of music in worship, and specifically in what we call the "church service"?

Let's first be sure to affirm that music does have a place in our worship services. And both Testaments do affirm that fact.

> Praise the LORD!
> Sing to the LORD a new song,
> And His praise in the assembly of the saints.
> > –Psalm 149:1

Praise the LORD!
Praise God in His sanctuary;
Praise Him in His mighty firmament!
Praise Him for His mighty acts;
Praise Him according to His excellent greatness!
Praise Him with the sound of the trumpet;
Praise Him with the lute and harp!
Praise Him with the timbrel and dance;
Praise Him with stringed instruments and flutes!
Praise Him with loud cymbals;
Praise Him with clashing cymbals!
Let everything that Has breath praise the LORD!
Praise the LORD!

–Psalm 150

...be filled with the Spirit, speaking to one another in psalms and hymns and spiritual songs, singing and making melody in your heart to the Lord.

–Ephesians 5:18-19

Let the word of Christ dwell in you richly in all wisdom, teaching and admonishing one another in psalms and hymns and spiritual songs, singing with grace in your hearts to the Lord.

–Colossians 3:16

These passages make it clear that we are to use singing and all kinds of instrumental music, "in the sanctuary," "in the assembly of the saints," and "to one another." The Bible is not very prescriptive on this. It doesn't address the frequency with which we should use music. It certainly doesn't address style. But we should feel confident that when we worship together, declaring and expressing the greatness of God through music, we have the support of Scripture behind us. We might summarize the function of music in these passages this way: *music is a tool with which to express our devotion to God and to proclaim His works.*

Another story gives us a slightly different picture of the function of music in worship. In 1 Chronicles 15-16 we find the narrative of the restoration of the ark of the covenant to Israel. The ark, which is literally the seat of the presence of God, had fallen into Philistine hands. After Israel recaptured it, David purposed to bring it to Jerusalem to give it its proper place. He pitched a tent for it, and they brought it and set it up in its tent. And the Bible says that David:

> ...appointed some of the Levites to minister before the ark of the LORD, to commemorate, to thank, and to praise the LORD God of Israel: Asaph the chief, and next to him Zechariah, then Jeiel, Shemiramoth, Jehiel, Mattithiah, Eliab, Benaiah, and Obed-Edom: Jeiel with stringed instruments and harps, but Asaph made music with cymbals; Benaiah and Jahaziel the priests regularly blew the trumpets before the ark of the covenant of God.
> So [David] left Asaph and his brothers there before the ark of the covenant of the LORD to minister before the ark regularly, as every day's work required;
>
> –1 Chronicles 16:4-6, 37

It is clear from this passage that David and the Israelites thought it proper that music should accompany, or be used in response to, or hail the presence of God. From this we may conclude that *music is a way to respond to God's presence*.

Why Should We Use Music? From God's Perspective

We have just established that music is fitting for use in congregational worship. And we have established two functions of music in congregational worship, namely: (1) music is a tool with which to express our devotion to God and to proclaim His works, and (2) music is a way to respond to God's presence. Now we want to uncover some of the benefits of music in congregational worship (and in individual worship). Why should we use music? We'll begin by addressing this question from God's perspective. What does God get out of us using music?

Well, first of all, music is a gift from Him, and He has commanded us to use it. So our simple obedience in using music in worship brings glory to Him. Second, thinking back to our discussion of worship in Chapter 1, music is a creative act, and by participating in it, we are imitating God's creative acts. This imitation of God is worship, and He receives glory from it. Third and finally, God enjoys music. Some way or another—and we can't know how—God is a sensory Being. He does not have eyes, ears, and a mouth, the way we do. But the Bible does attribute these qualities, these anthropomorphisms, to Him (Deu 11:12, Psa 18:6, Isa 40:5). The Bible indicates that God can hear (2Ch 7:14), God can see (Gen 1:4), and God can even smell (Exo 29:18). And it is pretty clear from the totality of Scripture that He enjoys music.

Why Should We Use Music? From Man's Perspective

Now, what is it that *we* get out of using music in worship? Here are four reasons to worship through music-making:

1) Music is Transcendent. Music, like all the arts, allows us to express something that cannot be expressed any other way. This is actually the purpose of art. There are just some things that cannot be expressed in words. That's why nonverbals are such an important part of communication. Similarly, paintings, sculptures, poetry, drama, music, and many other artistic avenues, allow us to transcend the more easily recognizable communicative routes (that is, words) to allow our souls, even our spirits, to express themselves to God.

When used appropriately, in holiness and in worship, this transcendence allows us to connect with God more deeply.

2) Music is Emotional. For many, this is seen as a negative. But that is a skewed perspective. Yes, we do want to avoid *emotionalism*, where we are more interested in being moved emotionally than we are in actually following the Lord. But that doesn't mean we aren't emotional. God created us as emotional beings, and He expects us to get emotional, particularly when we are in communion with Him. It is absolutely ridiculous to think that a son of God could go through life without engaging the Father on an emotional level. And music helps us to engage with emotion. Just think about watching a tense dramatic moment in a film at a time when there is no music, and then a lone violin enters on a single sustained pitch. That single pitch can totally shift the temperament of the soul to bring an emotional charge to the experience. In the same way the incorporation of music into worship can lift our spirits and help us to emotionally engage our God. I've often said that singing a song of worship is the quintessential act of fulfilling the greatest commandment (Luk 10:27). Through the lyrics we worship Him with our *minds*, through our voices we worship Him with our *strength*, through the act of devotion and obedience we worship Him with our *hearts*, and through the music we worship Him with our *souls*.

3) Music is Cultural. The Body of Christ is one, and we are called to unity. But most expressions of the body worldwide—local churches—are fairly homogenous in terms of culture. In each of these cultural pockets, music serves as a unifying force, contributing to the health and growth of the Body. For example, we don't generally program Chinese music at my church. That's because, since we have no Chinese people in our church, Chinese music would not help us connect to the lyrics, nor to each other. The music we program at our church speaks the language of our culture(s), and we are all able to engage with the music, the lyrics, and each other, as a result. Even in multicultural churches, which are possible in the West, the sharing of music from different cultures within a worship service can help us to celebrate our cultural distinctions, while at the same time celebrating the God who made us all unique. Through this celebration of diversity we can actually grow in unity.

4) Music is Practical. There is simply no better way to remember Scripture and theology than to set it to music. I have tried to teach my boys Bible verses by spoken memorization, and it is always such a long process. But the Scripture songs I have put in their ears, they have memorized in no time. The books of the Bible? They sing them in order. The practicality of memorizing good doctrine through music simply cannot be understated.

BENEDICTION

Heavenly Father, at the end of a book such as this, it is fitting to stop and turn our attention toward You, and worship You. You are the Beginning and the End. There is no one like You. From You and through You and to You are all things. That is why You will ultimately receive glory from your created order. You created us, not because You were lonely or had need of our worship or our service, but because You are so loving that You simply desired to share your effervescent love with us. For us who have been redeemed and reconciled, receiving your love and sharing it with others brings You glory. And that is your plan and purpose in creation.

We thank You for your Son, Jesus, through whom You made a way for us to worship You acceptably. Lord Jesus, You are the image of the invisible God, and in seeing You, we have seen the Father. Thank You for humbling Yourself and coming to earth to do what only You could do, die for us, and give us eternal life. We know that our worship is only acceptable if it is offered through You.

Father, we desire to worship You with the appropriate dispositions of wonder, adoration, and gratitude. And we ask You to transform our hearts to consistently see You in these ways.

We will praise and worship You according to the biblical mandates You have given us. We will clap, we will shout, we will sing, we will play instruments, we will bow, we will kneel, we will raise our hands, we will glow with the radiance of your glory. And we will serve You and serve others. We will declare our love for You, and we will express our love to You. But we will also take the more difficult step of demonstrating to You, in reverence and servitude, that You are worth more to us than is anyone or anything else.

We recognize that without holiness, our worship is unacceptable. We ask You to empower us by your Spirit to live lives that are pleasing to You. We consecrate ourselves to do our part. We start today by setting our minds on the things above, and not on the things on earth. We trust You to pick up from there, transforming our hearts as only You can.

Oh, merciful God, do not let us be deceived! Surround us with trusted friends and leaders who can bring correction and spiritual clarity into our lives. Help us to escape the traps that are so easy to get ensnared by, and to maintain a true faith.

As we seek to worship You through the gift of music, let us do so without pretense. Let us use music as You intended it to be used. Let our songs be pleasing sounds in your ear. Let them minister to You, and in turn, be moved by them to minister to us according to our needs.

Let the worship of God arise in these last days as it never has before. Let us, from this moment forward, fulfill our purpose with a zeal and effectiveness not seen in many generations. Make us true worshippers, *Soli Deo Gloria*.

NOTES

[1] John C. Lennox, *Seven Days that Divided the World: The Beginning According to Genesis and Science* (Grand Rapids, MI: Zondervan, 2011), 29.

[2] A.W. Tozer, *The Knowledge of the Holy* (New York: Harper Collins, 1961), 1-4.

[3] I say "son" here, with the understanding that both male and female believers in Christ are sons. The New Testament affirms this in many instances. "Blessed are the peacemakers, for they shall be called sons of God" (Mat 5:9). "For as many as are led by the Spirit of God, these are sons of God" (Rom 8:14). And on and on. This is important, primarily for one reason: throughout Scripture—from the physical of the Old Testament to the spiritual of the New Testament—we see that sons are the ones who receive the inheritance (Gal 4:7).

[4] David Peterson, *Engaging with God: A Biblical Theology of Worship* (Downers Grove, IL: InterVarsity Press, 1992), 97.

[5] Anselm, *Book of Meditations and Prayers*, trans. from the Latin by M.R. with a preface by His Grace the Archbishop of Westminster (London: Burns and Gates, 1872); 19th Meditation,

"Of the sweetness of the Divine Majesty, and of Many other Things." I. *Wonder at the unspeakable goodness of God the Creator, and the deep misery of man the creature.*

[6] Karl Barth, *Church Dogmatics*, III/2 (1960), reprint ed. (Louisville, KY: Westminster John Knox Press, 1994).

[7] Anselm, *Book of Meditations and Prayers*, 14th Meditation, I. *Of the wonderful being of God.* Edited by the author for flow.

[8] Augustine, *Confessions*, trans. E.B. Pusey (A public domain book), Book VIII par. 1. Edited by the author for flow.

[9] This story has been related in several sources.

[10] That is, in the King James Version. All statistics on the various frequencies of translations given in Chapters 5 and 6 refer to the King James Version, and have been accessed at www.blueletterbible.com.

[11] All definitions given in Chapters 5 and 6 are taken from the *Brown-Driver-Briggs* and *Gesenius* Lexicons, both of which are available from various online sources.

[12] John Wesley, "On Sin in Believers," in *The Sermons of John Wesley: A Collection for the Christian Journey*, ed. Kenneth J. Collins and Jason E. Vickers (Nashville: Abingdon Press, 2013), 565.

ACKNOWLEDGEMENTS

Abba Father, thank You for calling me to write this book, and for revealing to me the thoughts You desired to communicate through it. It is written for You. Use it for Your glory.

My wife, Samantha, and our boys have given me the time and space to write, with no complaints. They are the best family a man could hope for. Thank you so much for supporting me through this project. Mom and Dad, thanks for giving me the foundations to be able to grow into an understanding of biblical worship. To Fred Guilbert, thank you for seeing in me what wasn't yet there, and for the constant encouragement in spite of what was. To Dennis Dunn and the wonderful folks at River Outreach Church, thank you for giving me the opportunity to grow as a worship leader. Vernon Whaley, John Kinchen, and Paul Randlett, you have encouraged, challenged, and empowered me, helping shape me as both a worshipper and a teacher of worship: thank you. To Jeff, Bud, Adam, and my spiritual family at All Peoples Church, thank you for your trust, counsel, and support. And thank you for allowing me a platform to develop and communicate many of the ideas in this book. Thanks also to APM for the opportunity to publish.